The Ultimate Guide to Manifesting the Love of your Life!

Magical
Beautiful
Ride

By Cassandra Lea Wilson

ISBN# 978-1-988949-07-9

Published by One Day Publications

Artwork and Interior by Author

Cassandra Lea Wilson
cassandra@diamondsuccesscoaching.com

~ ~ ~

This creative work book is dedicated to those who seek and find love, a strong, lasting, loyal and abiding love, from here to eternity.

~ ~ ~

Acknowledgements

I want to thank all the people who have shown me love. I have been blessed to be loved by very special people who have enriched my life, starting with my father and mother, and brother and sister, and friends all over the world. But mostly, I want to thank those who have shown me what beautiful, romantic love is. Very much thanks to my true love for loving me no matter what.

Table of Contents

Introduction — Page 7
Tropical New Beginnings Love Story — Page 11
Day 1: This Love is Destined — Page 13
Day 2: Let's Get it! — Page 15
Day 3: Letter to Myself — Page 17
Day 4: The Bathtub Sanctuary — Page 19
Day 5: Feel Joy — Page 21
Day 6: 3 New Things — Page 23
Day 7: Visualize — Page 25
Day 8: 3 Things to Stop — Page 27
Day 9: Family Themes — Page 29
Day 10: Promises — Page 31
Day 11: Sacred Space Realm — Page 33
Day 12: Emotional Scale to Joy — Page 35
Day 13: Conflict Resolution Tactics — Page 37
Day 14: 3 Olive Branches — Page 39
Day 15: Opportunity to Clear Your Heart — Page 41
Day 16: Visualize Often — Page 43
Day 17: Feng Shui - The Ancient Art of Placement — Page 45
Day 18: Prior Commitments — Page 47
Day 19: Crystal Work — Page 49
Day 20: Chakra Balancing — Page 51
Day 21: Clarity Vision Board — Page 53
Day 22: Top 10 Things — Page 55
Day 23: List of Things for You — Page 57
Day 24: Favourite Things — Page 59
Day 25: Fun Things to Do — Page 61
Day 26: Letter to my Partner . — Page 63
Day 27: Your Love Story — Page 65
Day 28: Rest and Be Found — Page 67

INTRODUCTION

HELLO TRUE LOVERS AND TWIN FLAMES!

It's time to celebrate! You have found the exact workbook to take you on a Beautiful, Magical Ride - a love journey like no other. I'm so excited about the love you are going to create in this workbook, and also for the old energy you are about to release! You have made the move to open your heart and welcome real love.

You are ready! You are ready for real love, lasting love and you have come to this book by divine destiny. This book is opening a new world for you, and its time. It's the perfect time for you to allow your inner lover to arrive.

You are ready! Congratulations!

This journey to your heart of love is going to delight you, excite you, fill you with energy and enthusiasm, increase your happiness and clear the way for new, greater feelings of love to enter. You are the magician here! And this is your magical tool to walk you through the necessary steps on the journey to an open heart and a willingness to receive a love that does you justice.

Over the next 28 days, you will walk through your desires like you are walking through a garden. Pick the flowers, smell the roses, let the sunshine kiss your face and nourish you, while you luxuriate in all the ways love enters your life.

How did I get here and why did I write this book?

My name is Cassandra Wilson and I am passionate about Love - how to live it, how to allow it, how to receive it, and how to give it. Love has always intrigued me since I was a child, wondering about whom I would marry. I'm an energy worker, alchemist and personal development and true love coach, published author, teacher/ student, and the creator of the True Love Creations brand. It is my purpose to teach Love and to help us open our hearts to receive love and to sing in the glory of bliss. I am obsessed with enlightenment and feeling total Joy in life!

I created this 28 day ritual because I saw so many people who needed help to clear their hearts and welcome love, and so many of them seemed lost upon the path. We have become deluded on our paths to love in this busy world when what we really want is deep, abiding love with sweet, fresh and light days to fill our hearts with Joy.

If you were raised witnessing tumultuous or non-existent relationships, or got your romance from television, join the club. So many of us have not had good role models when it comes to having love or manifesting a relationship of our dreams.

Wherever you are on your love journey, it's time to take stock. Perhaps you've dated and not found lasting love, or you've been hurt, you need help to get you over this hurdle.

True Love to the rescue!

The Universe has put this book in your hands for a reason, because my way of looking at love and working through the blocks against it, will work for you. I've manifested beautiful loving relationships and I've also been hurt. But I persevered and even met my twin flame! I am choosing to live with my true love in happiness while I build my love energy and help my twin flame, as well.

My goal is to help you find real love. This carefully created workbook was downloaded to me in one fell swoop, when I was ready to receive a key tool to help others connect with their true loves and twin flames. It can be done. You can start believing right now.

The only challenge you have is to believe as I walk with you through the pages. You may not even believe there is a way right now, but that's the perfect reason to start now. That belief won't change unless you do something about it. And buying this book is a powerful shift!

You may believe that love is possible but all of the possibilities seem endless. So many choices and so many possibilities. This book will help you narrow down your choices and decide what it is you want, and even better it will help you create the visual pictures of what you desire so that you even know what it looks like! Your heart knows the way and this book will help you remember what you need to find your love.

The magical turnkey within this book is *the time you invest* for the next 28 days, completing one page a day. Use the bordered page next to it for your notes, drawings, mantras, affirmations, or to glue on pictures, talismans or feathers you find along your way. Feathers are from the angels letting you now that they are with you, helping you. If you find feathers, be sure to glue them in to the pages you are working on when you find them.

Each page takes between 10 - 30 minutes to complete, and each page is a step up toward the altar of Ultimate Love. As you complete each page, check the box. Do the workbook front to back. Place it under your bed in between uses. Imagine you are walking up the steps as you finish each day. If you miss a day, don't worry as the amazing Universe may be working to realign circumstances. Just start again as soon as you can to keep the momentum going which signals the loving Universe of your powerful intent! In Love, Cassandra.

Imagine... You're on a tropical beach, having swam there after your ship capsized. You find this book while searching for some food to sustain you. You sit down on the sand, and open the cover.

It's a book of love letters. As you read each page you imagine the beautiful love that caused this man to write this woman, and if they were still on the island. You stand up and begin to walk down the beach. You wonder if anyone is on this deserted island. But then, you see smoke and a campfire.

Then, a man comes out of the forest and stares at you. He looks familiar and your heart skips a beat. He looks stunned to see you, then begins to run toward you with a big grin on his face, his arms open wide.

You feel something magical is taking place and you relax to see him coming toward you. You're moments from your embrace when you finally recognize his eyes and you open your arms to him.

Welcome to your dream life.

This workbook in your hands is your magical tool of creation. The pages within are where you will imagine and create the love life you most want to live. You will explore your feelings, your heart and mind, and memories to create a living, breathing scrapbook of your creation of love.

In between each decorative page to help you build your dream life, there are blank pages for you to use however you would like. You can use them as scrapbook pages by gluing photos or affirmations, mantras or promises. You can draw or write, or work out your thoughts on these pages. They are meant to support you and so they are left blank for your unique creation experience. Check the box on the table of contents when each page is completed. You can finish them in your desired order or by following the table of contents.

I recommend storing this book under your bed in between uses and when its complete so it can help your dreams to manifest and give you clues in your waking life.

Enjoy your journey into ever greater love.

This isn't just
any love.
This is true love.

True love
is the love you set out
in advance of this life.
This partnership
is destined.

Let's Get It!

Let's get real! This is your life we're talking about! You deserve happiness, love, security, affection, and a loving partner! Let's take some time to think about what's important for you. Answer these questions below in writing or think about your answers and write them later.

What are your goals in partnership?

What are your key objectives for a lifetime partnership?

At the end of your life what is going to be important to you?

What are your fears about manifesting this partnership?

Where are your personal boundaries that you want respected?

Where is the space in your life for love to blossom and grow?

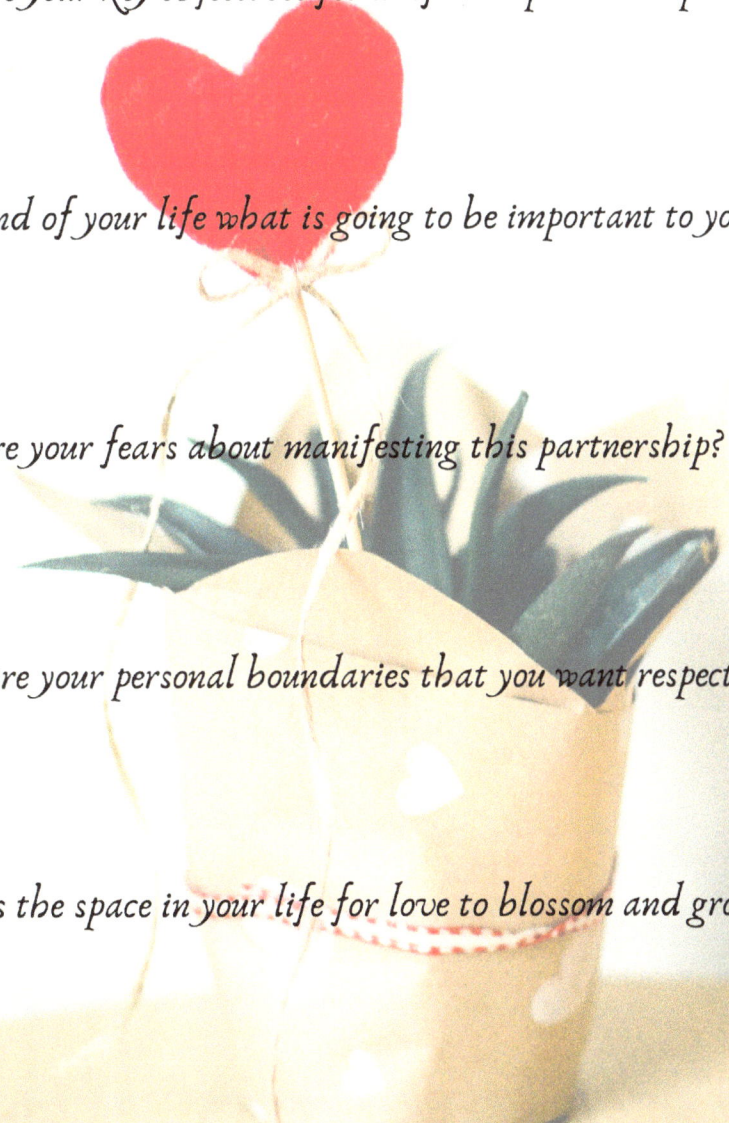

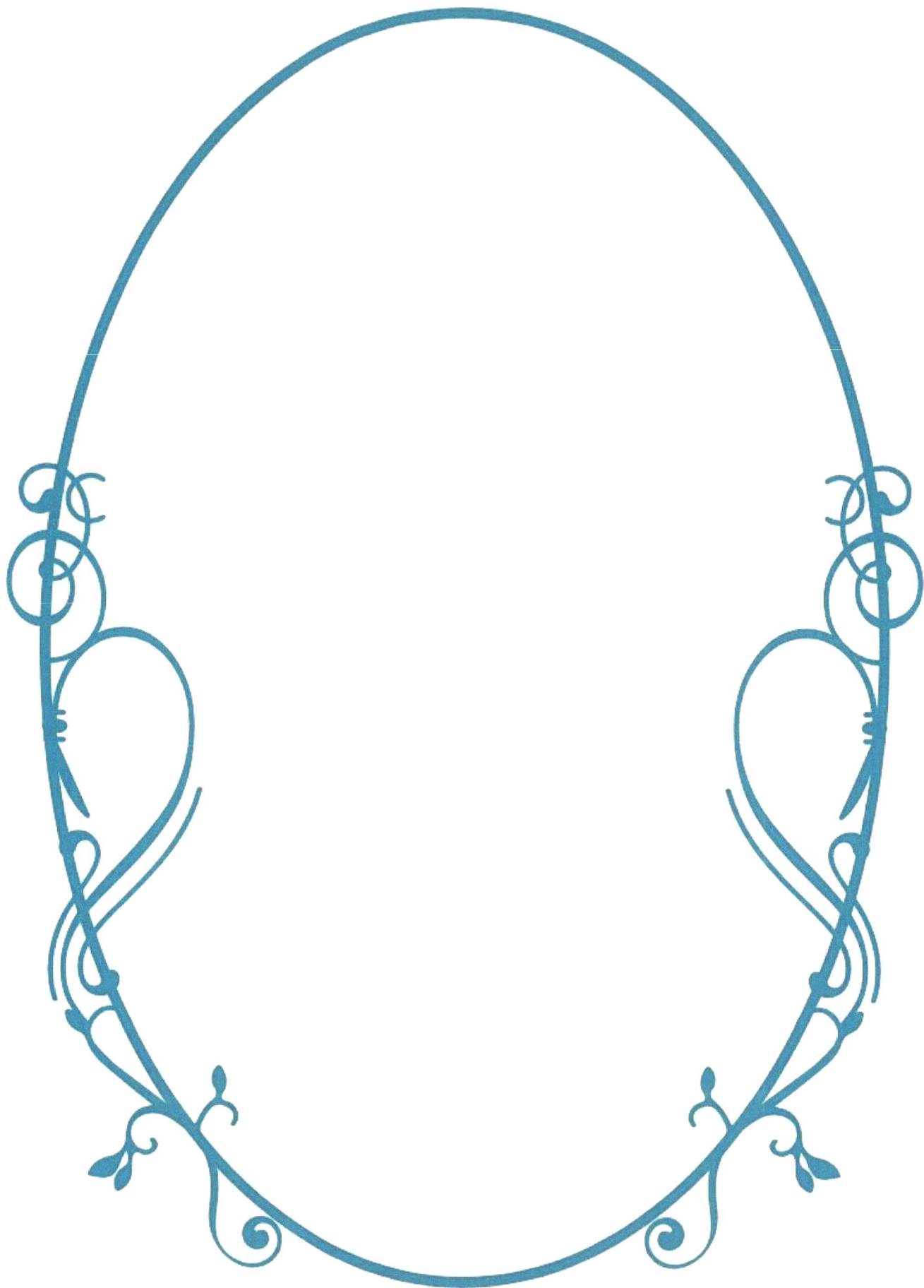

Letter to Myself

_____

_____

_____

_____

_____

_____

_____

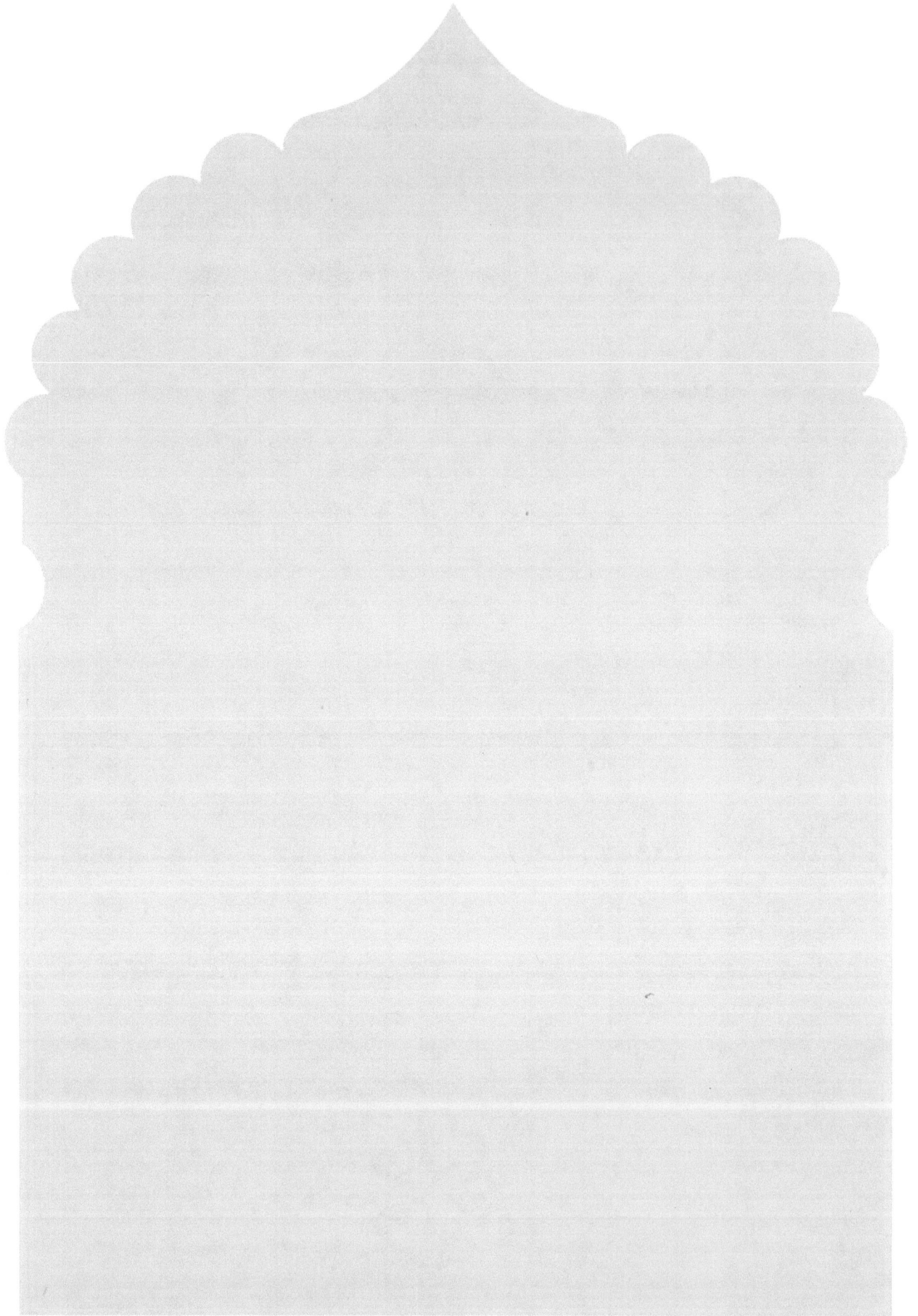

The Bathtub Sanctuary

Make a date with your bathtub, often. Light some candles, pour some bubble bath and maybe a glass of wine. Soak into the azur waters, freeing your mind and your spirit. Let the tranquil waters envelop you. Take a deep breath and blow it out then just relax. This is your special, sacred time. Just let your mind go where it wants to go - imagine your future, reminisce on your past. Listen to the meanderings of your heart, the wanderings of your mind. Are you inspired to reach out to someone, get back in touch, or maybe call someone for the first time?

Let your intuition speak to you during your bathtub moments where often times the barriers are down, your walls recede into the distance, and your heart opens To hear the whispers of your soul. This is the space where your intuition can speak to you. Make sure to act on the Nudges after you get out of the tub.

Feel Joy as you do these things

- Go shopping for wedding dresses

- Choose your engagement ring

- Create a wedding scrapbook

- Plan your honeymoon

- Write your committment vow

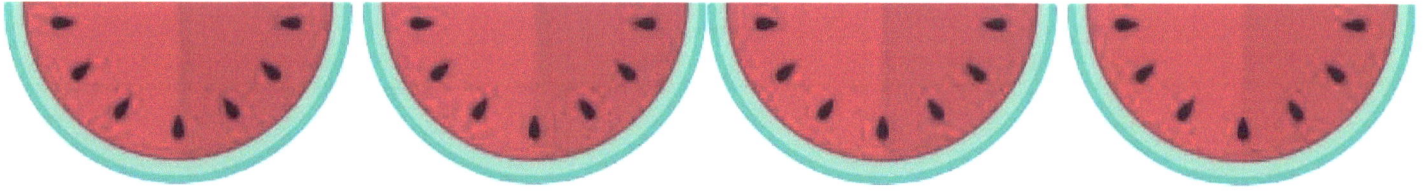

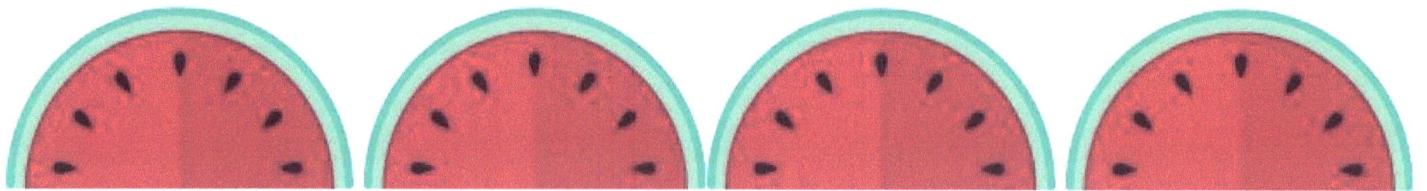

What are *3 new things* you'd like to start with your beloved?

1

2

3

Visualize

Close your eyes and imagine these scenes... often.
FEEL what it feels like, and let the feelings linger...

How does your beloved wake you up in the morning?

What is your nightly ritual?

Where do you travel together?

What does it feel like
in your beloved's embrace?

Three things I need to stop doing
in my dating life:

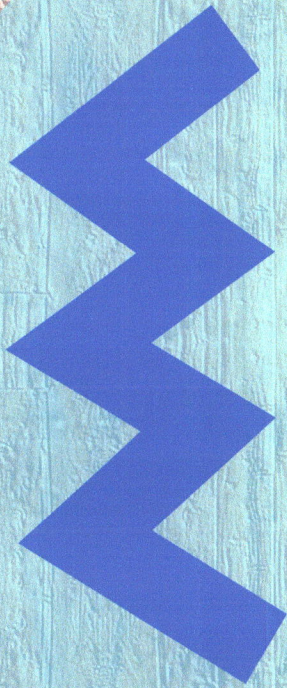

I promise to love these things about myself
And grow into something better.

Family Themes

Often times, because of the way of the family lineage, issues that are unresolved in our ancestors are passed down through the genes so that we have an opportunity to heal that in our family line. They say when we heal an issue that has plagued our family for generations, it heals the future generation and also those in the past.

When you look at your family history including the words of your relatives, what are your opportunities to heal family struggles in love? It may be that you indeed have to work to heal one of these issues in your love life. Consider the relatinoship issues you may be faced with as you search for your ideal partner. Endeavour to heal genetic stories with wise new choices.

Write the issue you want to heal horizontally. Write the healed issue vertically.

Promises

What are some of the promises
You want to make?

What are some of the promises
You want to hear?

Sacred Space Realm

Do this when you have some quiet time. Light a candle. Sit in your favourite comfy chair. Close your eyes.

Imagine your perfect match sits in a chair across from you. Witness him or her silently. Then, silently speak your truth to them. Tell them your hopes and dreams for your partnership, your fears, and how you would like them to help you.

Then, tell them how excited you are to meet them and you look forward to that very soon.

Write your impressions, experience or insights inside the box.

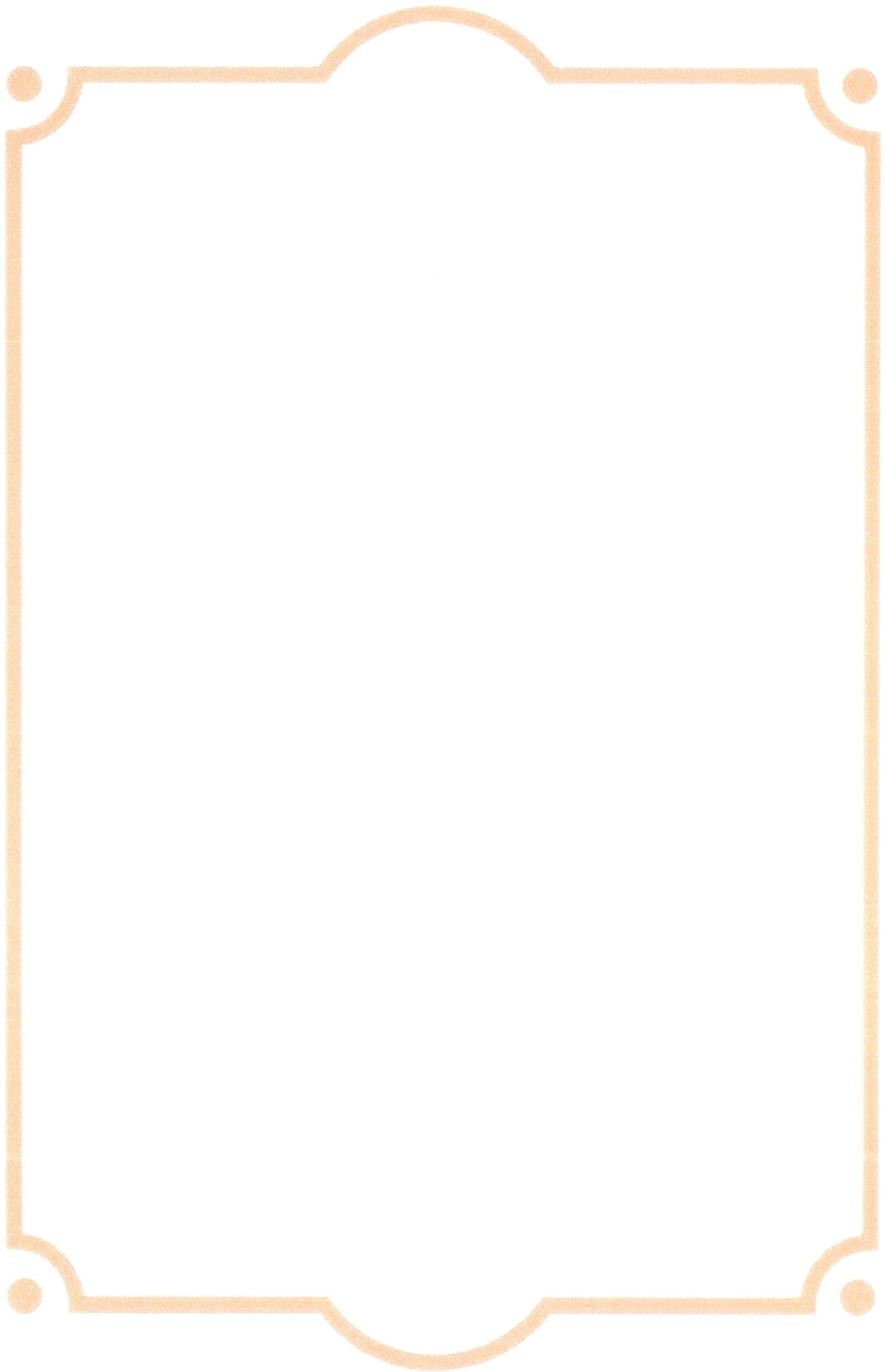

The Emotional Scale

This is the list of emotions. You will feel some or all of these emotions during your life. At that time, they would be Your Emotions. No one can make you feel anything unless you allow yourself to feel it. Take responsibility for your emotions at all times because it is only you who has power over your thinking and to change how you feel. Use your thoughts to create mental pictures you want to experience, not those that make you feel worse. If you want to feel better, intend to move up the emotional scale, one step at a time. Identify your current 'range of comfort' and endeavour to move your range up toward Joy, until you feel Joy often. Make some personal notes alongside the emotions listed as you take a general overview look at your emotional range. Place a sticker or draw a star beside the emotions you want to feel.

Joy/Appreciation/Empowered/Freedom/Love

Passion

Enthusiasm/Eagerness/Happiness

Positive Expectation/Belief

Optimism

Hopefulness

Contentment

Boredom

Pessimism

Frustration/Irritation/Impatience

Overwhelment

Disappointment

Doubt

Worry

Blame

Discouragement

Anger

Revenge

Hatred/Rage

Jealousy

Insecurity/Guilt/Unworthiness

Fear/Grief/Depression/Despair/Powerlessness

Conflict Resolution Tactics

Use these tactics every time you have a disagreement so that you can resolve
them with love, deepening your understanding and compassion for each other.
Share your answers too if you wish.

1. If I were in your place, I would think/feel/know

_____

2. If I had to defend you in your position, I'd say

_____

3. If I had to forgive you for any of the above, I would because

_____

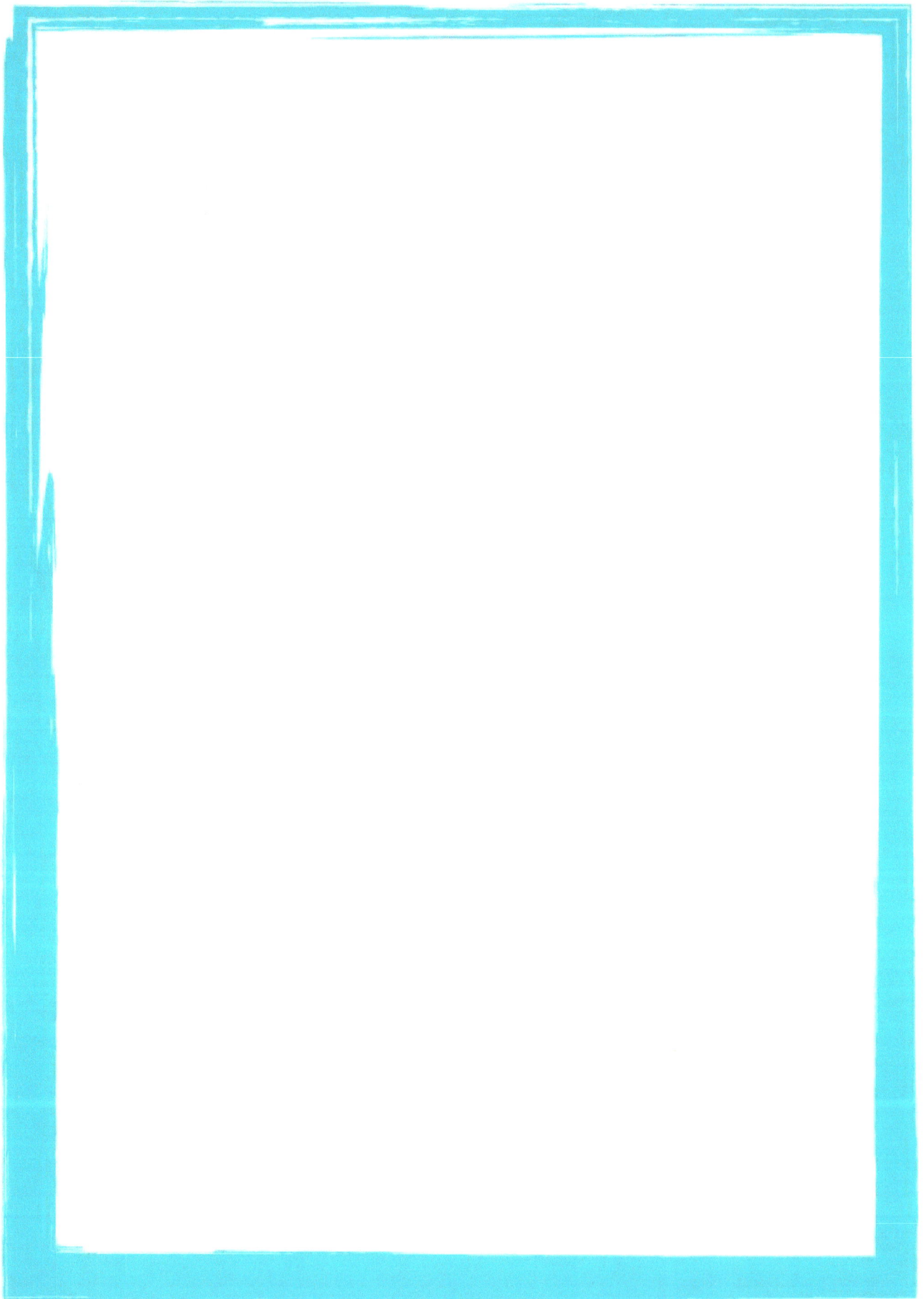

3 Olive Branches

Describe, post an image or draw 3 things you can do to bring you back together after feeling or being apart.

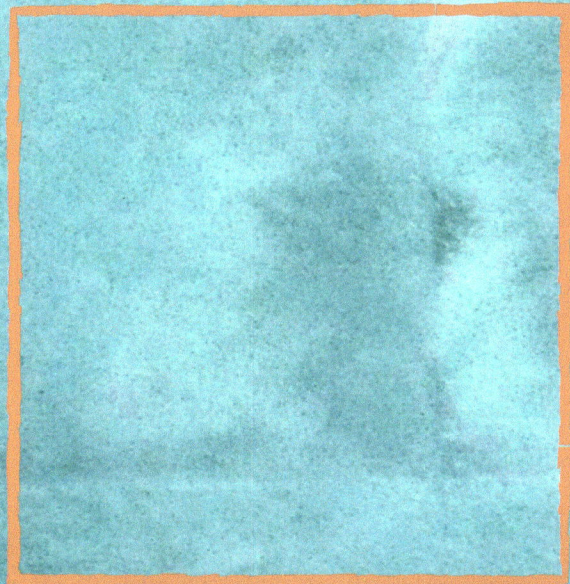

Opportunity to Clear your Heart

Write down three conflicts or situations you've had in your life that have hurt you, that you feel you may be still holding onto. Can you acknowledge how you may still be holding these wounds and how that may be keeping you from love. Let's resolve those now.

Let's begin. Close your eyes and feel this pain or sadness in your body. Remember the story of what has happened that hurt you. It may feel heavy right now. Inhale white light and blow out blue light onto these feeling experiences. Continue to inhale white light and blow out the blue light onto these emotions. Pay attention to any images that come to your mind.
See the blue light changing and transmuting the energy of density in your emotions. If you see an image and this could be an image from your past, blow blue light onto it.
Keep inhaling White Light and blowing blue light until it feels better.

Use this strategy of white light turning into blue light and breathing this blue light on your challenging emotions. This is a strategy you can use for many things in your life. Write down your positive impressions and experiences after you complete your session.

You may also use tapping or EFT as a solution creator for these trapped emotions.

Visualize Often

My perfect life

My perfect meeting of my partner

My perfect relationship

My perfect wedding

My perfect married life

My perfect achievements
after marriage

How it feels when we've found each other

What does it look like on holidays

I am already experiencing this wonderful life as my higher self. I feel as if its already happened!

Believe!

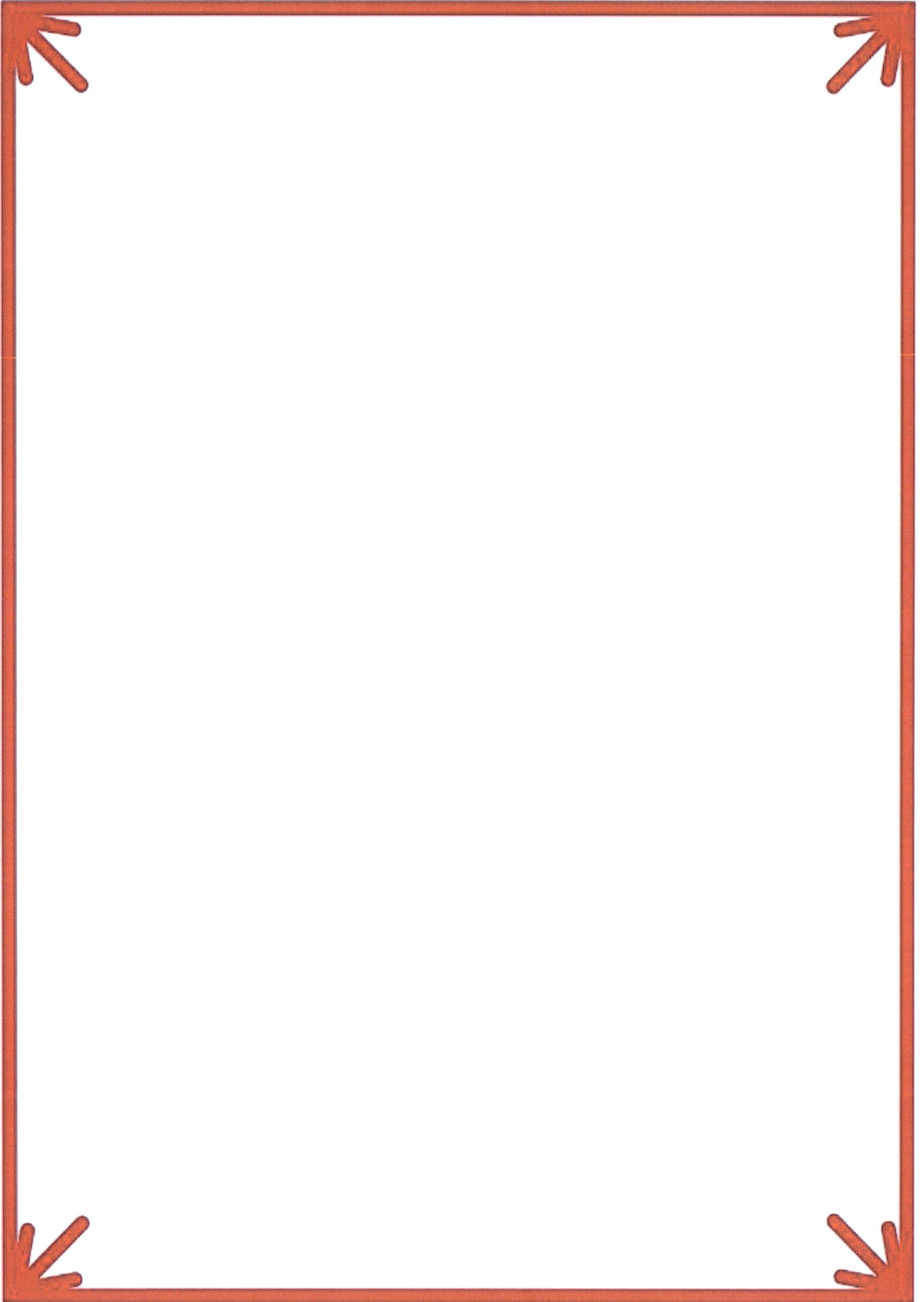

Feng Shui -
The Ancient Art of Placement

Decorate your home and bedroom with the principles of feng shui principles that set the stage for love. Try these changes!

* Decorate in pairs
* Have 2 night tables, one on each side of the bed.
* Hang paintings of bird pairs
* Arrange your things neatly
* Put out a new welcome mat!
* Freshen up bedsheets
* Remove stuffed animals
* Use romantic artwork
* Make your bedroom a sanctuary
* Remove photos of friends or family in bedroom
* Use Yin energy and art
* Use pink or red candles safely in the bedroom.

Prior Committments

If you feel unable to commit or allow true love, consider past
vows of celibacy, chastity or marriage vows you may have made.
Ask your angels and spirit guides to help you release those
agreements that no longer support you.
Imagine you place all the vows you have made upon a table.

Douse the vows in your imagined blue light. Separate the ones
that serve you from the ones that do not, creating two piles.
Bless the pile on the left as vows you choose to keep. And use
the Violet flame for the vows on the right that you choose to
transmute into a higher vibration. Visualize the Violet flame
burning the old vows that no longer serve you.

Imagine yourself in a wedding dress. Look down at the fabric
and design. Do you have any emerging feelings?

If your gown is white and glowing, and your shoes are suitable,
you are ready.
If you have mixed feelings, sit with them.
Allow the stories into your mind as they unfold for you.
Listen, bless and release anything that is in need of letting go.

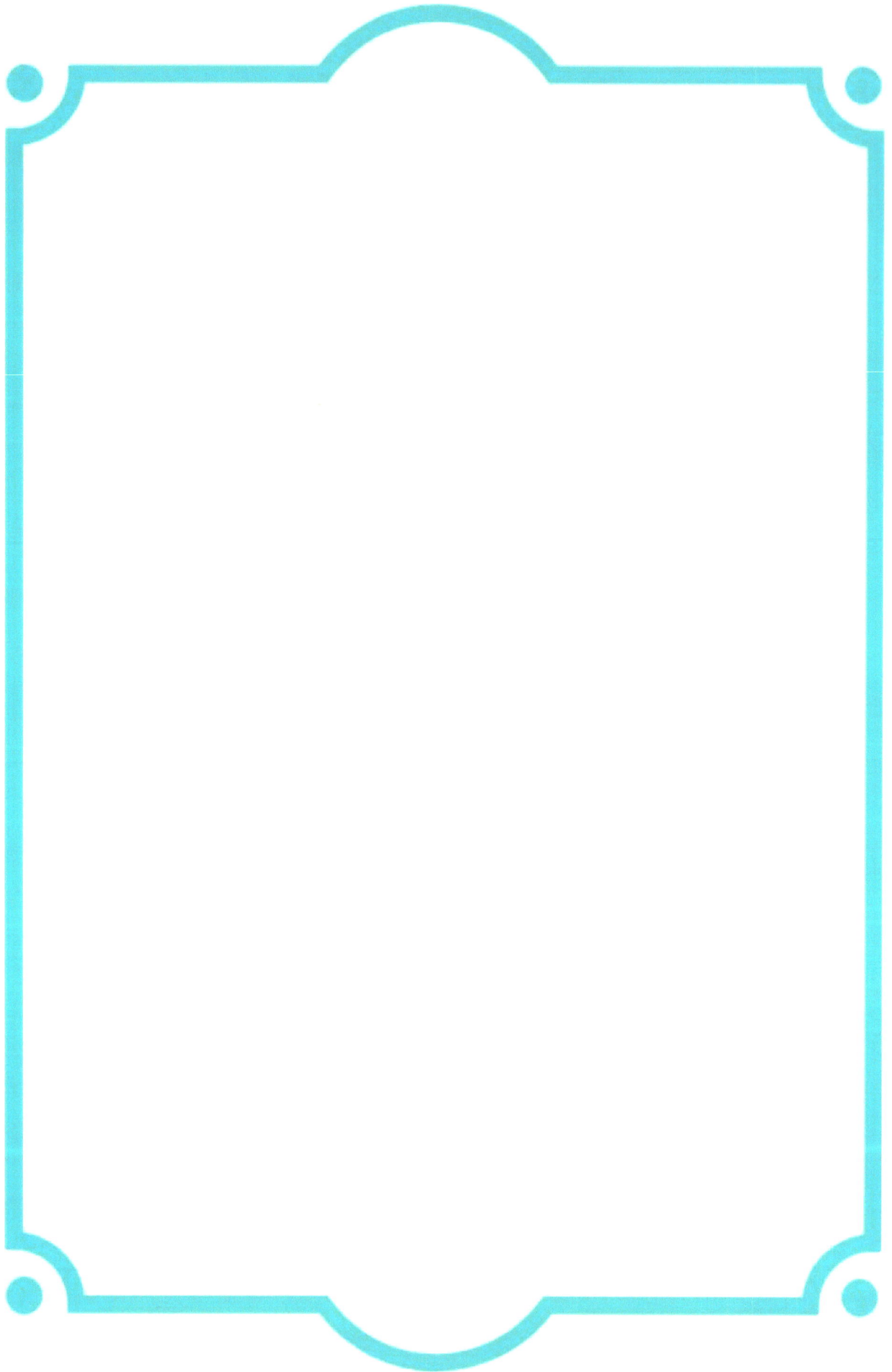

Crystal Work

Crystals are high vibe rocks. They can hold energy, transmute energy and clear energy. It is important to wash them and keep them clean, charging them up with sunlight or moonlight in between use.

You can use crystals in many ways. Here are a few ways you can use them in your Love Life. Make a note about the crystal's work in your life.

1. Vibrate a new reality. Hold one or more in your hand and close your fingers around it. Imagine your ideal Love scene, the next one you have in mind: meeting your true love, a love interest asking you on a date, or your true love asking for your engagement. Impress the energy and imagery of the scene into the crystal and ask it to hold the vision for you. Place the crystal where you will see it, as it pulses out your vibratory desire. You will await that vision coming true.

_____

2. Clear an emotion. If you are feeling a lower scale emotion in your tummy or elsewhere in your body, place the crystal over the place where you feel the emotion. Hold it there as you imagine your emotion leaving your body and going into the crystal. It will absorb the emotion. When you feel better, fill the empty space in your body with light. Then wash the crystal and place it in sunlight or upon the earth to clear it.

_____

3. Expand an emotion. If you are feeling very happy and joyful, hold the crystal and place some of your joyful feeling into the crystal to hold it and vibrate it for longer into your life.

_____

Chakra Balancing

Chakra balancing is a great way to clear old energy, old emotions and energetic shadows from your body. Its like taking your body through a car wash.

The Method

Find 7 handheld crystals to work with. If you don't have crystals, now is a good time to buy 7 small ones. They are very affordable at your local gem shop. Wash and clean them and charge them with sunlight.

When you are ready, close the door for some privacy, light a candle, play some soft music and lay on your bed. Place the crystals along the top of your body in the middle. Ideally, place them over your 7 chakras, from darkest to light. One each over your Root, Sacral, Solar plexus, Heart, Throat, Third eye, and Crown chakra which is above your head.

Once the crystals are placed, start by focusing on the lowest one, the root chakra's crystal. Do some breathing, back and forth, and imagine your breathes are mopping out the round energy centre that is your root chakra inside your body. Take twelve breathes back and forth to clear the chakra. The crystal will help absorb any negative energy and expand the positive qualities of the clearing. Once you have finished the first root chakra, move upward, one chakra at a time using your breath to clear the energy. Go all the way up with twelve inhalations and exhalations. When you get to the crown chakra, finish your 12 breaths and relax. When you feel ready, collect the crystals gently and blow on them to cleanse them in gratitude for the clearing. You may feel lighter, so be gentle with yourself. You could take a bath or sit in nature to ground your new, clearer self!

Notes:

_____

_____

_____

For more information there is a Blog on our website about Balancing your Chakras. DiamondSuccessCoaching.com

Clarity Vision Board

The purpose of a vision board is to draw in your creative energy and Decide on your desires. In this world of shiny objects, it can be a challenge to decide. This exercise will help you focus on what you are really wanting. What do you want?

The easiest way to create a vision board is to go to canva.com and build a desktop picture vision board by using their library of photos and uploading photos from google. In their user friendly design website you will be able to easily create a picture image of what you want. Use it to create a vision for your Love Life. Where do you want to travel to? What are the experiences you want to share? What do you want your coupledom to look like?
Creating a visual reminder of your desires helps you to focus on what you truly want. And by doing it online then saving it to your desktop, you can change it or tweak it when you would like. You could also do it by collecting magazine images and making a collage. It's up to you.

1. Go to canva.com

2. Choose desktop picture template.

3. Go to the sidebar into photos.

4. Type the word of the image you want to add and double click on it.

5. Size it and move it on your template.

6. Continue to place all relevant photos in your template.

7. Fill the template with images or use a background.

8. Download and save it to your photos.

9. Load the photo as your desktop picture!

Top 10 things
I *want you to do for me*

_____

_____

_____

_____

_____

_____

_____

_____

_____

_____

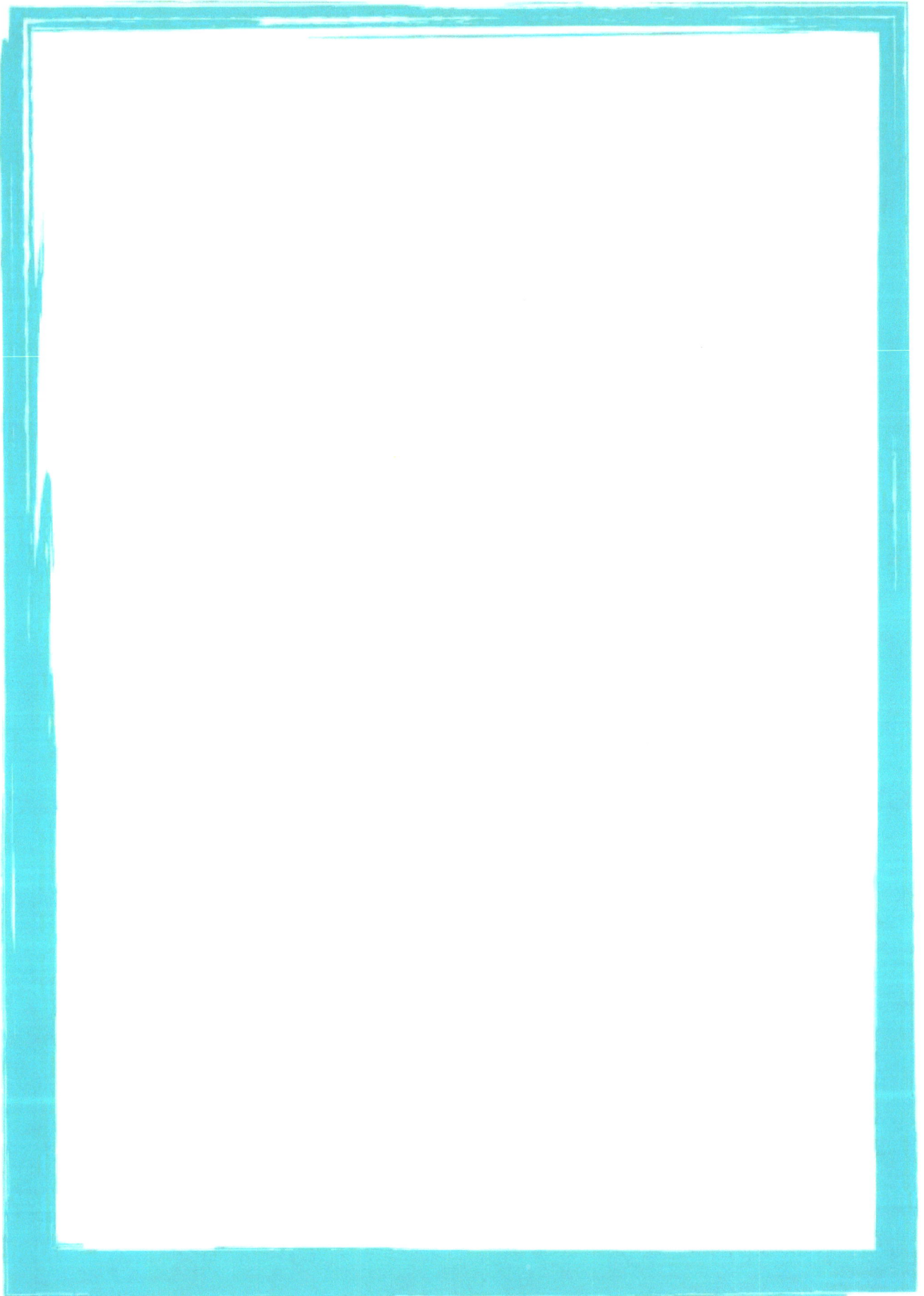

List of Things
that you want me to do for you

To be filled out by your future partner

Favourite Things

What are the favourite things you want to do together? Make a list of seven things inside the bubble that you want to do together and describe it. This will help you shape your experiences and adventures.

Fun Things to do!

* Make a mantra to read to yourself every day. Write it on a cue card and decorate it.

* Make a vision board that displays your experience of true love.

* Make a list of three traits your true love will have and place them on your vision board.

* Make a playlist of romantic music that you will play with your true love.

* Imagine holding hands, kissing, hugging, laughing, discussing, eating, playing, going to bed, sleeping and waking up with your true love.

* Find or buy a ring to wear that signifies the space holder for your future partner.

Letter to My Partner

Your Love Story

Write or tell your love story and place it here. Imagine you are a novel writer, and you are describing your love story. Use romantic imagery, and involve all five senses: sight, taste, scents, touch/textures and sounds. Make it beautiful as if you would just love to live it! This is just for fun but it will help you create the vision. How do they meet? What does he say? What does she say? Where do they plan to meet next? What does he bring her? How does it unfold? How do they decide to be together? How do they enjoy everyday? What happens in five years? What happens in ten years? What are their proudest accomplishments? How do they spend their lives? What legacy do they create? How do they grow old together? See the elderly couple with a smile on their faces and hearts full of happiness and Joy. Read this beautiful story often, perhaps before bed as you drift into imagination creation.

Sign Your Name

Now, you can rest.

Imagine and visualize the Gifts he will bring to you.

Imagine what he may have been saving for this special moment of meeting you, and for a lifetime together.

Imagine how much he yearns to meet you.

Imagine his excitement building in his heart to be able to call You, his Love.

Open your heart, and await. He will make his way to You. He can hear you on the ethers. He knows he has to get to you, to find you.

The man is usually in search of the woman. So now, all you have to do is Be Found.

Enjoy this space filled with Love.

This book is a powerful, amazing tool to take you on a Magical Beautiful Ride. And may the love that follows also be a Magical Beautiful Ride through life.

CONGRATULATIONS!

You have manifested more love in your life! Receive the Love you have created and thank the Universe and yourself for following through!

You are a creator and there is nothing standing in your way for you to create the love life of your dreams.

Read your completed book often and revisit the pages to make sure you are very clear in your intentions. Unleash your creative energy toward your vision. There are plenty of good people waiting to meet you.

This book has helped you set the framework and grow your ability to feel and receive love! Say YES! to feeling and receiving more Love!

Practice feeling your enthusiasm and excitement for when you are living what you have created here. Hold the vision and keep your positive expectation. The Universe delivers!

I'm so happy and proud of you now that you have completed the workbook, invited love, and that you're feeling better! You deserve all of this and more!

In Love,
CASSANDRA WILSON
Author and True Love Creations Brand Creator
www.diamondsuccesscoaching.com